BEST RIDDLE BOOK EVER

Charles Keller
Illustrated by Jeff Sinclair

Sterling Publishing Co., Inc.
New York

To Gabriel

I would like to acknowledge the help of and give special thanks to Steven Blance, Rhoda Crispell, Robert Farhi, Brenda Gordon, Keith Planit, and Philip Recchia.

Library of Congress Cataloging-in-Publication Data

Keller, Charles.
    Best riddle book ever / Charles Keller ; illustrated by Jeff Sinclair.
        p.   cm.
    Includes index.
    Summary: A collection of over 500 riddles on many different subjects.
    ISBN 0-8069-9545-9
    1. Riddles, Juvenile. [1. Riddles. 2. Jokes.] I. Sinclair, Jeff, ill. II. Title.
PN6371.5.K3825   1997
818'.5402--dc21   97-11724
                                                              CIP
                                                             AC

10 9 8 7 6 5 4 3

First paperback edition published in 1998 by
Sterling Publishing Company, Inc.
387 Park Avenue South, New York, N.Y. 10016
© 1997 by Charles Keller
Distributed in Canada by Sterling Publishing
% Canadian Manda Group, One Atlantic Avenue, Suite 105
Toronto, Ontario, Canada M6K 3E7
Distributed in Australia by Capricorn Link (Australia) Pty Ltd.
P.O. Box 6651, Baulkham Hills, Business Centre, NSW 2153, Australia
Manufactured in the United States of America

Sterling ISBN 0-8069-9545-9 Trade
                 0-8069-9546-7 Paper

Contents

1. Fun Daze

What telephone number does a pig call when it gets into trouble?
Swine one one.

Where do farmers leave their pigs when they come to town?
At porking meters.

What happened to the pig in the hot kitchen?
It was bakin!

Why did the weary traveler burn down his house?
He yearned for home cooking.

Why did the chef's spaghetti fall apart?
He forgot the tomato paste.

When does Dracula find time to eat?
During his coffin break.

What do you get when you cross a tramp with a mummy?
A bum wrap.

Why didn't the melon get married?
Because it cantaloupe.

What do you call a rich watermelon?
A melonaire.

How do they get the water into the watermelon?
They plant them in the spring.

What do you call a duck that steals from banks?
A safe quacker.

If people live in condos, where do ducks live?
In pondos.

Why does an elephant have a trunk?
So he has something to hide behind when he sees a mouse.

How can you tell if an elephant has been using your toothbrush?
It smells like peanuts.

What kind of insect can't say yes or no?
A may-bee.

What did the bee say to the flower?
"Hey, bud, what time do you open?"

What do bees say when they come home?
"Hi, honey."

What time is it when a lion comes to dinner?
Time to go.

What did the lion cub say to its mother?
"Every day I love you roar and roar."

What would you get if you crossed a lion with a watchdog?
A very nervous mailman.

What's a great white shark's favorite game?
Swallow the leader.

What did the shark say when it bumped into the dolphin?
"Whale I didn't do it on porpoise."

What does the "Jaws" candy bar cost?
An arm and a leg.

How do dogs get rid of dog pounds?
They go on a diet.

Where do young dogs sleep when they camp out?
In pup tents.

What do you put on top of a doghouse?
A woof.

How do you cheer a basketball team?
"Hoop, hoop, hooray!"

What does a baby do when it plays basketball?
It dribbles.

What would you get if you crossed a groundhog with Michael Jordan?
Six more weeks of basketball.

Why did the rabbit cross the road?
To get to the hopping mall.

What do you do when you see a kidnapping in the park?
Wake him up.

How did the judge find out about the rotten milk?
There was odor in the court.

What did the judge do when he sentenced the
author?
He threw the book at him.

What do aliens use to tie up spacemen?
Astro-knots.

What kind of music do angels listen to?
Soul music.

Why did it take Brahms five years to compose his lul-
laby?
It kept putting him to sleep.

What famous musical composer invented the meal
you take on picnics?
Bach. He invented the Bach's lunch.

Why doesn't a frog jump when it's sad?
It's too unhoppy.

How do you get a frog off the back window of your car?
Use the rear defrogger.

Why is an old car like a baby?
It never goes anywhere without a rattle.

What would you get if you crossed a bridge with a car?
To the other side.

What do trees do for fun on weekend nights?
Hold a lumber party.

What do trees shout at races?
"We're rooting for you."

What did the tree surgeon say to the diseased tree?
"Your bark is worse than your blight."

Why did the fireplace call the doctor?
Because its chimney had the flu.

What do you call a group trip for physicians?
A doc tour.

What did the seasick passenger say when asked if they could bring him anything?
"Yes, bring me an island."

Why did the customer decide against buying a motor boat?
No sail.

Why do birds fly south for the winter?
It beats waiting for the bus.

What do baby birds call their parents?
Mother and Feather.

Why did the bird have so much energy?
It was standing on the power line.

2. Out on a Whim

What TV channel do horses watch?
Hay B.C.

What would you get if you crossed a horse with a kangaroo?
Built-in saddlebags.

What do horses put on their salad?
Mayo-neighs.

Where does a salad dressing get a good night's sleep?
On a bed of lettuce.

What did the cook say to the salad?
"You're old enough to dress yourself."

Why does a ghost get upset when it rains?
The rain dampens its spirits.

What's white and black and blue all over?
A ghost that can't walk through walls.

What would you get if you crossed a ghost with Bambi?
Bamboo.

What do you call a strange-looking female deer?
Weirdo.

Why did the boy deer propose to the rich female deer?
He wanted the doe.

What do you call a male moose after a long bath?
Bull wrinkle.

Why did the young bug run away from home?
It wanted to join the flea circus.

Why did the worm cross the road?
The chicken was chasing it.

What do they use for windows in a hen house?
Pullet-proof glass.

What do you do when a chicken starts to talk about eggs?
Drop the subject.

What size T-shirt do you buy for a 200-pound egg?
Eggs-tra large.

Why didn't the elephant cross the road?
It didn't want to be mistaken for a chicken.

Why do elephants prefer peanuts to caviar?
Peanuts are easier to get at the ballpark.

Why didn't the silly baseball player go to home plate from third base?
There was a masked man there.

What player on a baseball team pours lemonade?
The pitcher.

Why did the baseball rookie have coal on his face?
He just came up from the miners.

What did the police do when they thought Mark stole a watch?
Question Mark.

How did the police know the parrot was telling the truth?
They gave it a poly graph.

What would you get if you crossed a monster with a parrot?
I don't know, but you'd better bring it a cracker if it asks for it.

Why did the cucumber hire a lawyer?
Because it was in a pickle.

Why didn't the pickle like to travel?
It was a jarring experience.

What do you call a pickle that can add, subtract, multiply and divide?
A cuculator.

How did the tomcat find out he was a father?
His wife sent him a litter.

Why didn't Tabby have any friends?
She was too catty.

What magazine do cats like to read?
Good Mousekeeping.

What do cats call mice on rollerskates?
Meals on wheels.

How are hay and mice alike?
Catt-ll eat 'em.

What is Mickey Mouse's favorite car?
A Minnie van.

What did the teacher say to the french fries that were slow learners?
"Ketchup."

What school do you go to to learn to greet people?
"Hi" school.

Why did the students eat the math test?
The teacher told them it was a piece of cake.

Why do fish swim in schools?
Because group rates are cheaper.

What would you get if you crossed a salmon with a feather?
A fish that is pickled pink.

Which is more nutritious, a hamburger or a shooting star?
A shooting star, because it's meteor.

What's the fastest way to get to the moon?
Climb up on an elephant's trunk and tickle him.

Why shouldn't you put your foot in your mouth?
You'll get a sock in the jaw.

What does a leg wear to keep warm?
A knee cap.

Why were feet invented?
To give people a place to put their shoes.

What did Benjamin Franklin say when he discovered electricity?
Nothing. He was in shock.

How did the inventor discover gunpowder?
It came to him in a flash.

Who was the smartest inventor?
Thomas Edison. He invented the phonograph so people would stay up all night and use his light bulbs.

How do chess players tell bedtime stories?
"Once a-pawn a time."

What would you get if you crossed a soda with a waterbed?
A foam mattress.

When do old clocks die?
When their time is up.

What do you call an unemployed jester?
Nobody's fool.

What do comedians use to discipline their children?
Slapstick.

What do they write jokes with?
A puncil.

What did one pencil say to the other?
"Please get to the point."

What is filled with ink and has no hair?
A bald-point pen.

Why do salmon swim upstream to spawn?
Because walking on the riverbanks hurts their tails.

Why did the fisherman destroy his polluted car?
His Mercury was filled with tuna.

3. All in Fun

What happens when a ghost haunts a theater?
The actors get stage fright.

What did the ghost say to her daughter when she got into the car?
"Fasten your sheet belt or you'll go flying out the window."

What did the gingerbread man have on his bed?
Cookie sheets.

What does a baker do when he wants to sleep late?
He puts a "Doughnut Disturb" sign on his door.

What would you get if you crossed a Scottish monster with a watch?
The Clock Ness Monster.

What's the fastest thing in the world?
Milk—it's pasteurized before you see it.

Why does a milking stool have only three legs?
The cow has the udder one.

Why did the cow cross the road?
She wanted to moo-ve.

Why did the hippo stop using soap?
Because it left a ring around the river.

What did Noah say when all the animals were on the ark?
"Now I've herd everything."

What did the calendar say to the director of the marching band?
"March fourth!"

What would you get if you crossed TNT with old songs?
A blast from the past.

Why do they call the new dance the elevator?
It has no steps.

What's an avoidance?
A dance for people who hate each other.

How do you trip the light fantastic?
Stick out your foot.

What dance do opticians attend?
The eye ball.

Why was the chiropractor upset?
All he got from his patients was back talk.

Why were the teeth afraid of the dentist?
They were yellow.

When shouldn't a mountain climber yell for help?
When he's hanging by his teeth.

How did the mountain climber feel when he tumbled off the cliff?
Crestfallen.

What do you call a person who does arithmetic and scores touchdowns?
A mathlete.

What kind of clothes does a house wear?
A coat of paint and address.

What's the worst kind of clothes to buy?
Permanent mess.

What's tan and furry?
A peanut with a mink stole.

What's big, has a trunk and likes peanuts?
An oak tree with a squirrel in it.

How are a talk show host and a squirrel alike?
They both gather 10,000 nuts.

Where does a squirrel keep its winter clothes?
In a tree trunk.

Why is it better to have a tree than a dog?
A tree's bark doesn't bother the neighbors.

Why did Silly Billy mistake a dog for a tree?
Because of its bark.

Why don't dogs like to travel on planes?
Because they suffer from jet wag.

Where do airline pilots keep their money?
In cloud banks.

What did the firefly say when it boarded the plane?
"Bye, I'm glowing now."

What did the mother firefly say to her children?
"Lights out by midnight."

Why don't centipedes play football?
By the time they get their shoes on, the game is over.

Why is baseball like a pancake?
They both start off with a batter.

Where does a baseball player like to stay?
At home.

Why is it hard to be a turtle?
You can't run away from home.

What happens when you electrify a turtle?
Shell shock.

How did the snail cross the road?
He hitched a ride on a chicken.

How does a chicken tell time?
One o'cluck, two o'cluck.

Why are chickens such big eaters?
Because they eat a peck at a time.

Why did the chicken go out in the raging storm?
It was foul weather.

How do they find nettles in the woods?
With a nettle detector.

What illness do racing drivers get?
Indygestion.

What kind of tax does a hitchhiker pay?
Thumb-tax.

How can you tell that an elephant is on your head
during a hurricane?
You hear his ears flapping in the wind.

How can you tell that an elephant is living in your
house?
By the enormous pajamas in your closet.

How do you tell an elephant from a banana?
*Try lifting it. If you can't get it off the ground it's probably
an elephant. Although it might be a heavy banana.*

What fruit can tease you?
A ba-na-na-na.

What's green, red, and yellow and goes up and down?
A pickle, a tomato and a banana riding in an elevator.

Why did the girl go out on a date with an apple?
It had a peel.

What does a lobster give its teacher?
A crab apple.

4. Happy Campers

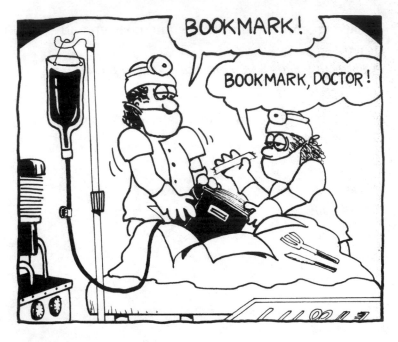

Why did the doctor operate on his medical book?
To take out its appendix.

Why did the bones chase the skull?
They wanted to get ahead.

What's the best place to see a monster?
From half a mile away.

What position does a monster play on a soccer team?
Ghoulie.

Why did it take the monster two months to finish the book?
It wasn't hungry.

What book has the most stirring chapters?
A cookbook.

Did the chef relax when he went out west?
Yes. He was home on the range.

What do you call a drop-dead hamburger bun?
A roll model.

Who saw the Brontosaurus enter the restaurant?
The diners saw.

What did one dinosaur fossil say to the other?
"I haven't seen you in ages."

Why did the dinosaur laugh so loudly?
It was pre-hysterical.

Why did the man cross the hyena with the parrot?
So he could find out what it was laughing about.

What do you say when you walk into a store the same time as a sheep?
"After ewe."

What do you get from iron-rich sheep?
Steel wool.

What did one grumpy sheep say to the other?
"Baa-humbug."

Who was Scrooge?
The Wizard of Blahs.

Where do polar bears vote?
At the North Poll.

How do you make bears listen?
Take away their B's and they are all ears.

Why do elephants have big, ugly, gray trunks?
Because Noah's laundry ran out of bleach.

When is an elephant like a cute little bunny rabbit?
When he's wearing his cute little bunny rabbit suit.

Why do rabbits hate Elmer Fudd?
Because he bugs bunnies.

What does a magician need when he loses his rabbit?
A hare restorer.

What happened when the two rabbits got married?
They lived hoppily ever after.

What is it called when two spiders get married?
A webbing.

What's the difference between mice and rice?
You can't throw mice at weddings.

What do cats like on a hot day?
An mice cream cone.

What's another name for a cat's house?
A scratch pad.

What's stranger than seeing a catfish?
Seeing a goldfish bowl.

What happened when the cat swallowed a ball of yarn?
She had mittens.

What animals are weight watchers?
Fish; they carry their scales around with them.

Why shouldn't you pollute the ocean?
Because you make the sea sick.

What do you take for motion sickness on a cruise?
Vitamin sea.

How do you know when the ocean is friendly?
It waves at you.

Why did the cactus cross the road?
It was stuck to the chicken.

Why do chickens make poor employees?
They are cluck watchers.

What did the boy egg say to the girl egg?
"Shell we dance?"

What do you call a mother that eats a lot of eggs?
A momelet.

Why didn't the omelet laugh?
It didn't get the yolk.

What would you get if you crossed an earthquake with a chicken?
Scrambled eggs.

Why did the comedian become a surgeon?
He always left his audience in stitches.

What famous inventor loved practical jokes?
Benjamin Pranklin.

What do you call an astronaut getting into trouble?
Astronaughty.

Why did the astronaut visit the doctor?
To get a booster shot.

What's an astronaut's favorite bar on the computer?
The space bar.

Why wouldn't the cleaning lady operate the computer?
She didn't do windows.

What happens when a dirty computer dies?
It bytes the dust.

What do you call it when a computer falls through the ice?
A breakthrough in modern technology.

How do you clean the ice off tall buildings?
With sky scrapers.

What should you do if you are carried out to sea on an iceberg?
Keep cool until rescued.

What did one knee bone say to the other knee bone?
"Let's get out of this joint."

Why did the skeleton cross the road?
To get to the body shop.

Why didn't the skeleton pass the test?
He didn't have any brains.

5. At Wit's End

What kind of fruit is never alone?
A pear.

What's green, grows on trees and is terrified of wolves?
The Three Little Figs.

What kind of tree has hands?
A palm tree.

What do you say when you want to stop a boat?
Whoa, whoa, whoa the boat.

What does a tugboat use to buy things?
A barge card.

What do ships eat for breakfast?
Boatmeal.

What do Parisians make before drinking champagne?
French toast.

What month is good for toast?
Jamuary.

What tastes better before it is cooked?
Burnt toast.

What's the best way to keep a barbecue fire hot?
Keep it coaled.

What do you call a single piece of firewood?
A mono-log.

How do you carve a statue out of wood?
Whittle by whittle.

Who tells long, boring stories about the forest?
Smokey the Bore.

How are Hansel and Gretel after surgery?
They're not out of the woods yet.

Why did little Miss Muffet need a road map?
She lost her whey.

What kind of cat comes with instructions?
A do-it-yourself kitty.

What did the boy cat say to the girl cat?
You look purr-ty.

What would you get if you crossed a cat with a shark?
A town without dogs.

What type of fish play poker?
Card sharks.

What did the fish say to the cat?
"Sorry, I can't stay for dinner."

How do you catch a school of fish?
With a bookworm.

What did the bus driver say to the fish?
"What school do you go to?"

What has eight arms and four wheels?
An octo-bus.

What driver never gets a ticket?
A screwdriver.

What kind of vehicle does a hog drive?
A pig-up truck.

Why did the pig cross the road?
It wanted to hear the cars squeal their brakes.

How do pigs wear their hair?
In pigtails.

What's a barbarian?
Someone who cuts your hair in a library.

Why are barbers always early?
Because they know the shortcuts.

Why did the two hairs say goodbye?
They knew they were going to be parted.

What bear loves to wash his hair?
Winnie the Shampoo.

What's the best way to hunt bear?
With your clothes off.

What do grizzly detectives look for?
The bear facts.

Why did the jockey cross a horse with a kangaroo?
So he could ride inside.

What would you get if you crossed a kangaroo with a cow?
A kangamoo.

Where does a cow get its medicine?
At the farmacy.

What medicine do you give a sick elephant?
Peanutcillin.

What do you give a angel to cure its flu?
A miracle drug.

What do you call it when cows and sheep go out all night to eat?
Star grazing.

Where do otters come from?
Otter space.

What kind of flowers grow in outer space?
Sunflowers.

What do you call someone who paints flowers?
A budding artist.

What did the grandma dandelion say to her grandson?
"My, you're growing like a weed."

Why didn't the flower go to school on its bike?
Its pedals were broken.

What do you call a meteor that doesn't hit the earth?
Meteorwrong.

What did the girl say when she decided to sell her bicycle?
"I think I'll peddle my bike."

What would you get if you crossed cactus with a bike?
A flat tire.

How do you change a duck's tires?
With a quacker jack.

Why did the goose cross the road?
To get a gander at the other side.

What did the goose get at bedtime?
A dressing down.

What case did the private eye fall asleep on?
The pillow case.

Where does a liar sleep?
In a bunk bed.

Where will campers sleep in the next century?
In the future tents.

What's another name for a suit of armor?
A knight gown.

What's the saddest part of the day?
Mourning.

What is an alarm clock?
Something that scares the daylights into you.

What gave the Wimbledon fan a headache?
The tennis racket.

What kind of policemen play tennis?
Members of the racket squad.

What do you serve that you can't eat?
A tennis ball.

Why don't fish play tennis?
They might get caught in the net.

Where do fish wash themselves?
In bass-tubs.

6. Jests in Time

What would you get if you crossed a potato and a frog?
A potatoad.

What do you get when you put a witch in the refrigerator?
A cold spell.

How do you make a witch itch?
Take away her W.

What kind of mail does a witch carry on her broom?
Hex-press mail.

What kind of mail flies?
Airmail.

How do they put out fires at the post office?
They stamp them out.

Who do firemen miss the most?
Their old flames.

What happened when the queen bee fell in love?
She got stuck on her honey.

Why did the bee go to the doctor?
It had hives.

Why did Mr. Potato Head refuse when the doctor wanted to give him artificial limbs?
He wanted to quit while he was ahead.

Why do potato farmers make good detectives?
They have an eye for everything.

What's the best way to buy alligators?
By the bog-full.

What happened when the skeleton fell into the swamp?
It was soaked to the bone.

What do New Yorkers wear in the rain?
City slickers.

When do bedbugs get married?
In the spring.

What's green and goes "clomp, clomp, clomp"?
A grasshopper trying out his new hiking boots.

What did the horsefly say to the blacksmith?
"Shoe me."

What did one shoe say to the other shoe?
"I'll run ahead and see what's underfoot."

What kind of shoe does a lazy person wear?
Loafers.

Why doesn't a guitar work?
Because it only knows how to play.

What did the guitar say to the rock star?
"Why are you always picking on me?"

Why do elephants trumpet?
They don't know how to play the violin.

What would you get if you crossed an elephant with a penguin?
An animal in a tight-fitting tuxedo.

What do you call an elephant that flies?
A dumbo jet.

What would you get if you crossed an elephant with a skunk?
I don't know, but you could smell it coming from miles away.

What would you get if you crossed a skunk with a porcupine?
A very lonesome animal.

And what would you get if you crossed a skunk with a boomerang?
A smell that keeps coming back.

What's black and white and blue all over?
A skunk at the North Pole.

What kind of paste do they use at the North Pole?
Igloo.

What do Eskimos order in delis?
Cold cuts.

Why did the frankfurter bun turn down offers from Hollywood?
The rolls weren't good enough.

What do you call a hamburger bun in a rocking chair?
Rockin roll.

Why did the meatball sandwich get a medal?
Because it was a hero.

What did the sneezing champion win at the Olympics?
The Cold Medal.

What did the father snowman say to his son when he got into the car?
"Don't turn on the heater!"

What does a nut say when it sneezes?
Cashew.

What's the only nut with a hole in it?
A doughnut.

What did the doughnut say to the cake?
"If I had your dough I wouldn't be hanging around this hole."

Why is a doughnut like a great golfer?
It has a hole in one.

Why did the golfer yell at his caddy?
He was teed off.

What's a golfer's diet?
You stick to the greens.

What do you call a cartoon expelled from school?
Suspended animation.

What does a dog get when he finishes obedience
school?
A pet degree.

If dogs go to obedience school, where do cats go?
Kittygarten.

Where do cats go on vacation?
To the meowtains.

How can you tell if a head of lettuce is reformed?
When it turns over a new leaf.

What did the boy say to the wormy lettuce?
"You should have your head examined."

Why did the gardener quit his job?
He didn't like the celery.

What do you call a tired gardener?
Bushed.

Where does a gardener learn his trade?
In nursery school.

Why did the aging climber refuse to scale the mountain?
He was already over the hill.

What's a computer sign of old age?
Loss of memory.

What ailment do computers get most often?
A slipped disk.

What does a computer do when it gets hungry?
It gets a byte to eat.

What do you call a horrible dream in which a were-wolf is attacking you?
A bitemare.

Why doesn't a vampire chew its nails?
Because they hold its coffin together.

What did the doctor advise the train conductor to do with his food?
Chew, chew.

Why did the old house go to the doctor?
It was having windowpanes.

Why can't you trust a man who works on a hillside?
He's not on the level.

7. Funny Bones

How do cows get rid of grass?
They moo it.

What is it called when cows help each other?
Cow-operation.

What did the cow say to the silo?
"Is my fodder in there?"

What did one scarecrow say to the other?
"Hey, man."

Why did the cowboy keep his horse in the barn?
He wanted to give it a stable environment.

Why is a cowboy a lot of laughs?
He's always horsing around.

Why did the pony think it could fly?
Because it saw the horsefly.

Why did the hen go to the doctor?
To get a chick-up.

What did the shepherd say to get the sheep's attention?
"Hey, ewe."

Where does a sheep take a bath?
In the baa-tub.

Why did the shower go on a diet?
It was getting tubby.

Why did the man eat the chandelier?
He was on a light diet.

Which one of King Arthur's knights weighed over 300 pounds?
Sir Lunch-alot.

What knight always ran out of gas?
Sir Gallon-had.

What would you get if you put a light bulb in a suit of armor?
A knightlight.

What did the happy lamp say to the grumpy lamp?
"Lighten up, will you."

What did the candle say to the match?
"You light up my life."

What light bulb asks a lot of questions?
A 100-watt bulb.

What travels 100 miles per hour underground?
A mole on a motorcycle.

What do you say to a burrowing animal that wins a race?
"Gopher it!"

What do you call rabbits that get divorced?
Splitting hares.

What did the beaver say to the chain saw?
"They're playing our song."

When is a piece of chicken like a musical instrument?
When it's a drumstick.

What musical instruments are like our bodies?
Our ear "drums" and our internal "organs."

What do pianos drink?
Hi C.

What juice do ghosts like?
Boo-berry.

What did the blueberries say to the girl who got all A's on her report card?
"Berry nice."

What do you call a duck that gets all A's on its report card?
A wise quacker.

What do you call a bunch of bees?
A good report card.

When does a "B" come after "U"?
When you disturb its hive.

What letter is envious of the rest of the alphabet?
Jealous E.

What do you call a 12-inch letter?
A footnote.

How many letters are in the alphabet?
Nineteen. Because E.T. went home on a U.F.O. and the F.B.I. went after him.

What kind of party do departing spacemen have?
A blast.

How can you tell if a planet is married?
It has a ring around it.

How did the TV set's wedding turn out?
The reception was great.

What do rocks watch when they can't sleep at night?
The Slate Show.

What do you call an artificial stone?
A shamrock.

What do you call a bunch of dancing pebbles?
The Rockettes.

Where do turkeys go to dance?
The Fowl Ball.

Why didn't the bicycle go dancing?
It was two tired.

What do you call a fast tricycle?
A tot rod.

Why did the boy construct a bicycle out of paper?
He wanted a stationary bike.

What did the paper say to the scissors?
"Cut it out!"

What did the paper and pen say to the ranch hand?
"Write 'em, cowboy."

What pen does a baby write with?
A play pen.

What type of writing does a waiter use?
A menuscript.

What does an envelope say when you lick it?
It just shuts up.

Why is it hard to understand zippers?
They only talk in zip code.

What travels all around the world yet stays in one corner?
A stamp.

How do telephone operators talk?
In dial-ect.

What do you call cheese that talks a lot?
Chatter cheese.

What's a scary kind of cheese?
Muenster.

What would you get if you crossed mozzarella with a clown?
A cheesy clown.

What happened to the human cannonball at the circus?
He was hired and fired on the same day.

How did the ditchdigger get his job?
He fell into it.

How do you confuse a ditchdigger?
Hand him two shovels and tell him to take his pick.

Why did the girl put lipstick on her forehead?
She was trying to make up her mind.

What do you call a dumb balloon?
An airhead.

What sign do you put on the top of a dummy's ladder?
"STOP."

8. Side Splitters

What did the teddy bear say after dining out?
"I'm stuffed."

What kind of arguments do dogs like at dinner?
Table scraps.

What do you call a monster with no neck?
The Lost Neck Monster.

What does a good-looking ghost look like?
It is very hauntsome.

What kind of heavy equipment does a ghost operate?
A boo-dozer.

What do you call a battle between two road-paving companies?
Tar Wars.

What did the sidewalk say to the jackhammer?
"You crack me up."

When does a truck driver stop to eat?
When he comes to a fork in the road.

Why was the little bird punished at school?
It was caught peeping during a test.

What did the student do when he lost his pen a second time?
Re-search.

At what college do soldiers learn to drive tanks?
Tank U.

Why was the farmer famous?
He was outstanding in his field.

Why did the farmer bury the chicken?
He wanted to raise eggplants.

What happened when Humpty Dumpty fell off the wall?
All the king's men had scrambled eggs.

Why didn't the turkey cross the road?
The Pilgrims were on the other side.

How do ducks celebrate special events?
With fire quackers.

What would you get if you crossed a canary with a hammerhead shark?
A bird that builds its own cage.

What would get if you crossed a magician with a photographer?
A lot of hocus focus.

What would you get if you crossed a dinosaur with a football player?
A running back that no one can tackle.

What's gray on the inside and brown on the outside?
A chocolate-covered dinosaur.

How do you keep bagels from being stolen?
Put lox on them.

How did the belt break the law?
It held up a pair of pants.

How many judges does it take to change a lightbulb?
Two. One to turn it and another to overturn it.

Why can't they keep people with allergies in jail?
They keep breaking out.

What do you call a frozen policeman?
A copsicle.

Why did the computer stay home from school?
It had a virus.

What dinosaur coughs the most?
The bronchitis.

What does Dracula take for a cold?
Coffin drops.

Why couldn't the viper vipe her nose?
Because the adder 'ad 'er 'ankerchief.

What does a girl snake give to a boy snake after their first date?
A good night hiss.

What do you call two oranges kissing?
An orange crush.

Where do we find mangoes?
Most places women go.

What's the most common ailment among grapes?
Clusterphobia.

When is a banana like an artist?
When it draws flies.

What do one bread crumb and another bread crumb equal?
A bunch of ants.

What did the windshield say to the bug?
"I'll bet you don't have the guts to hit me again."

Who are the most faithful insects?
Ticks. Once they find a friend they stick to him.

What do you do when your dog has ticks?
Don't wind him.

What did the second hand say to the minute hand on the watch?
"I think I'm lost—I keep going around in circles."

Why do we never have a minute to ourselves?
Because the minutes aren't hours.

Why did the watchmaker get a promotion?
He worked around the clock.

What do you call a man who washes whales?
A blubber scrubber.

Where does satisfaction come from?
A satisfactory.

Where do locksmiths go on vacation?
To the Florida Keys.

Why did the bald man have no use for keys?
He didn't have any locks.

What does an ear of corn have when it gets dandruff?
Corn flakes.

Who is the leader of the popcorn?
The kernel.

What did one potato chip say to the other?
"Shall we go for a dip?"

What do birds eat for dessert?
Chocolate chirp cookies.

What kind of bird goes to church?
A bird of pray.

Why do giraffes stand on their heads?
To trip clumsy birds.

What did the nearsighted gingerbread man use for eyes?
Contact raisins.

What did the ape say when it dialed the wrong number?
"King Kong ring wrong."

What did the monkey say to the vine?
"Thanks for letting me hang around."

What did the can say to the can opener?
"You make me flip my lid."

What did the tired dishcloth say to the counter?
"I'm wiped out."

9. Snicker Snacks

What does a ghost use to go hunting?
A boo and arrow.

What's the best place to keep your baseball mitt?
In the glove compartment.

What traffic violation is common in baseball?
Hit and run.

When does Dracula help a baseball team?
When he turns into a bat.

How do witches drink their tea when flying on their broomsticks?
Out of flying saucers.

What do you call a plate that is not truthful?
Dish-honest.

What did the broom say to the vacuum cleaner?
"People keep pushing us around."

What do you call a pretty girl using a broom?
Sweeping Beauty.

What did the Prince say to Cinderella at the ball?
"What's a nice girl like you doing in a palace like this?"

What boy puppet spins like a top?
Spinocchio.

How did the boy puppet get into show business?
His friends pulled a few strings for him.

Who was the first person to say T.G.I.F.?
Robinson Crusoe.

Who rides on a raft, hates school, and eats very little?
Huckleberry Thin.

What do you call a crazy baker?
A dough nut.

How can you tell when a watermelon is crazy?
When it's out of its rind.

How come only two elves can sit under a toadstool?
Because there isn't mushroom.

What does a frog build a skyscraper with?
Rivets, rivets, rivets.

What's a frog's favorite thing at Christmas?
Mistletoad.

How does St. Nick's wife feel at Christmas?
She Mrs. Santa Claus.

Who does Rudolph turn to for advice?
Deer Abby.

What kind of music is played at Santa's workshop?
Wrap music.

What kind of furniture likes pop music?
A rockin' chair.

How can you tell when a drummer is at your door?
The knocking never stops.

Why was the hockey player a success?
Because he was goal-oriented.

What kind of skates does a calculator wear?
Figure skates.

What unknown person has a lot of money?
John Dough.

What's the best pattern for a banker's suit?
Checks.

What's the best way to break a bad habit?
Drop it.

What's the best lubricant for fishing rods?
Castor oil.

Why is coal one of the best fuels ever used?
Because there is no fuel like an old fuel.

What do insurance companies pay you when you get
a bump on your head?
A lump sum.

Why do gymnasts go to taverns across the street from
each other?
Because they like parallel bars.

What's another name for choir practice?
Hymnastics.

What kind of dog makes you say "ouch"?
A Doberman pincher.

When is a storyteller like a happy dog?
When his tale is moving.

What do you call a person hit by a Wells Fargo wagon?
Stage struck.

What would you say if cannibals surrounded you and tied you to a pole?
"My life is at stake."

Why should you never upset a cannibal?
You might get into hot water.

What happened when the chimney got angry?
It blew its cool.

Why did the pig cross the road?
Because he was a road hog.

Where do you find a pig with no legs?
Where you left him.

What do you call a pig that is mean and nasty?
Dis-pig-able.

What would you get if you crossed a porcupine with a pig?
Splinters in your bacon.

What kind of shoes does a plumber hate?
Clogs.

What do you call a plumber's helper?
A drainee.

What dreams does a plumber have?
Pipe dreams.

What are the laziest coins?
Sleeping quarters.

Why did the exhausted robber hold up the bank?
He was hoping for arrest.

Why did the worm oversleep?
It didn't want to get caught by the early bird.

Why do smokers whisper?
Because smoking is not aloud.

What do you call a clone that chews tobacco?
A spittin' image.

How do spiders learn definitions?
They study the Web-ster dictionary.

What do you call an actor who performs outdoors?
Outcast.

What do you call an adult balloon?
A blown-up.

What do you call a polite butler?
A civil servant.

How do you keep a stiff upper lip?
Put starch in your mustache.

What are hippies for?
To keep your leggies up.

Why do elephants have round feet?
So they can walk on lily pads.

Why did the elephants laugh at Tarzan?
They thought his nose was funny.

Why did the elephant walk around in white socks?
Someone stole its tennis sneakers.

10. Laughing Out Loud

Why are the floors of basketball courts wet?
The players dribble a lot.

What kind of uniform do female basketball players wear?
Hoop skirts.

What do mice wear to play basketball?
Squeakers.

Why do elephants wear green tennis sneakers?
So they can tiptoe across pool tables without being seen.

What did they call elephants in ancient Egypt?
King Tusk.

What did one pyramid say to the other?
"How's your mummy?"

What do you call a mummies' convention?
A wrap session.

How did they know the invisible man had no children?
Because he's not apparent.

How did they know Dracula was broke?
He was always putting the bite on people.

How did the gambler feel at the racetrack?
Bettor.

What do you call a fast duck that always wins races?
A quick quack.

How do we know that dinosaurs raced professionally?
Scientists found dinosaur tracks.

Where do you find flying rabbits?
In the hare force.

If joy is the opposite of sorrow, what is the opposite of woe?
Giddyyap.

Why was the cow arrested?
She shot the bull.

Where do savvy cows make investments?
The livestock market.

Why was the banker upset?
He lost interest in everything.

Why are goaltenders thrifty?
Saving is their job.

How do you know when perfume is cheap?
When you get all you want for a scent.

Why should you save your pennies?
It just makes good cents.

What's the most expensive game of tag?
Price tag.

What's a milk carton's favorite game?
Follow the liter.

What do amphibians play late at night?
Sleepfrog.

What's the best hand for a cat to have in a card game?
A full mouse.

Why should you never wear a polka dot shirt when playing hide and seek?
Because you are always spotted.

What did the lioness say to the lion?
"It's so nice to have a mane around the house."

What did the bee say when it returned to the hive?
"Bee it ever so humble there's no place like comb."

Why does a turtle live in a shell?
Because it can't afford an apartment.

What do you call a kid's messy room?
A toynado.

How do you make the world go backwards?
Put it in revearth.

Where do bow ties go on vacation?
To Thailand.

Why did the leopard have a lousy vacation?
It couldn't find the right spot.

Why should beach-bound Parisians always carry sun-tan lotion?
Because French fry.

Why do people wear sunglasses?
Moon glasses are too dark.

What do you see on a clear day in California?
U.C.L.A.

What do you call it when the ocean is foggy and the grass is moist?
Murky sea, murky dew.

What's the difference between a gardener and a laundryman?
One keeps the lawn wet and the other the laun-dry.

Who does Santa Claus buy his gardening tools from?
Frosty the Hoeman.

What do you use to fix a broken ruler?
Measuring tape.

What do you call three feet of trash?
A junk yard.

What kind of necktie does a pig wear?
A pigsty.

Why did the garbage look sad?
Because it was down in the dumps.

Why was the fox upset?
Everyone kept hounding him.

How does Avis feel about being number two?
It Hertz.

What animal cries a lot?
A whale.

How did the girl feel when she swallowed the feather-filled pillow?
Down in the mouth.

How can you tell when a wedding cake is sad?
By its tiers.

When are your eyes not your eyes?
When the sharp wind makes them water.

Why didn't the girl look through the screen door?
She didn't want to strain her eyes.

What do you get when you put a jar of honey out overnight?
Honeydew.

What do hangmen read with their morning coffee?
The noose paper.

What newspaper do reptiles read?
The Scaly News.

Why don't cannibals eat the illiterate?
Because Readers Digest.

What does a singer need to become a opera star?
A real opera-tunity.

What did the musician call his concert of classical and modern music?
Bach to the future.

What do you get when you practice karate in the forest?
Chopsticks.

What do all boxers have in common?
A striking resemblance.

ABOUT THE AUTHOR

Charles Keller has been working and playing with comedy all his life. Working for CBS as a script consultant, he edited many of the great classic sitcoms, such as *M*A*S*H, All in the Family,* and *The Mary Tyler Moore Show,* and he also worked on other prime-time comedy shows. He got started writing children's books because he didn't like many of the ones he read and thought he could do better. Now, over 40 books later, he maintains the country's largest archive of children's rhymes, riddles, witty sayings, and jokes, and constantly updates his massive collection. When he isn't writing children's books, he can be found creating educational software for children. Born in New York, Charles Keller is a graduate of St. Peter's College. He presently resides in Union City, New Jersey.

ABOUT THE ILLUSTRATOR

Jeff Sinclair has been drawing cartoons ever since he could hold a pen. He won several local and national awards for cartooning and humorous illustration. When he is not at his drawing board, he can be found renovating his house and working on a water garden in the backyard. Jeff has gone into cyberspace on the Internet. He lives in Vancouver, British Columbia, Canada, with his wife, Karen, son, Brennan, daughter, Conner, and golden Lab, Molly.

Index